Who? What? Why?

Book I AD 60 to 1485

Philip Page

Edward Arnold

First published in Great Britain 1981
by Edward Arnold (Publishers) Ltd
41 Bedford Square, London WC1B 3DQ

Edward Arnold (Australia) Pty Ltd
80 Waverley Road, Caulfield East
Victoria 3145, Australia

Reprinted 1984

British Library Cataloguing in Publication Data
Page, Philip
  Who? What? Why?
  Book 1: AD60 to 1485
  i. Great Britain·— History – Juvenile literature
  I. Title
  941   DA30

ISBN 0-7131-0471-6

Set in Linoterm Plantin and printed in Great Britain by the Pitman Press, Bath

Contents

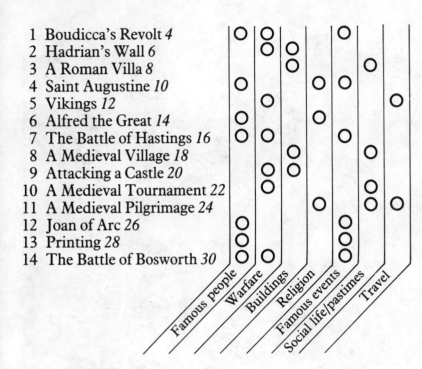

For the teacher

The chapters in this book cover some of the main events in British History between the years AD 60 and 1485. They are set out in chronological order and so may be followed through as a complete course.

However, the book will also be useful for those teachers who adopt a thematic approach. The subject matter of each chapter lends itself to the examination of a theme or themes and these may be followed by using the matrix on the left.

Each chapter forms a double-page spread, the left-hand page being an illustration, the right-hand page a passage of text followed by 'Things to Do'. Each illustration is designed to make the pupil study it closely before answering the questions based on it. Each 'Things to Do' section begins with a simple written exercise and questions based upon observation of the picture. The final exercise is designed to promote skills of empathy, drawing or further research.

There is a list of suggestions for places to visit at the end of the book.

4

1 Boudicca's Revolt

The Roman army invaded Britain in AD 43. Some of the British people soon began to copy the Roman way of life but others hated the Romans. Boudicca hated the Romans. She was the queen of the Iceni tribe which lived in the east of the country and the Romans had treated her very badly.

In the year AD 60 she and her tribe revolted and other tribes joined her. Her army destroyed the Roman town of Colchester and defeated one Roman army sent against her. She moved on and burnt down the other Roman towns of St Albans and London.

The leader of the Romans in Britain was Suetonius Paulinus and he had been in Wales with his army. Now he moved east to meet and fight Boudicca. He knew that if he did not defeat her the Romans might have to leave Britain. The two armies met at Mancetter, near Atherstone in Warwickshire.

In the picture the Britons have just charged on foot and in their chariots at the Romans. Now a Roman centurion has told his men to attack. They have thrown their javelins and have drawn their swords. In the distance are the wagons of the British army and they will get in the way of the Britons when they try to retreat.

The Romans won the battle and Boudicca took poison rather than be captured. The Roman soldiers killed every Briton they could find. It was the end of the revolt.

Things to do

A Write the heading **Boudicca's Revolt** in your books. Copy out this paragraph and fill in the missing words.

Boudicca revolted in the year AD _____. She was the leader of the _____ tribe. She attacked the towns of _____, _____ and _____. The leader of the Romans was called _____ _____. He and Boudicca fought a battle at _____ in what is now Warwickshire. Boudicca lost the battle and took _____ to avoid being _____.

B Answer the following questions by looking at the picture.
1 What are the differences between the centurion's armour and that of his men?
2 What has happened to the javelins that the Romans have thrown? Why do you think that they were designed to do this?
3 What is the broken object in the front of the picture at the right? What is it made of?
4 Describe the weapons that the Roman soldiers are using.
5 Look at the dead and injured Britons. In what ways are they not as well protected as the Romans?

C These are the Latin (Roman) names for some of the Roman soldiers' equipment. Draw a picture of each of them and write their names by them.
gladius (sword), scutum (shield), pilum (javelin), pugio (dagger), cassis (helmet), caligae (sandals).

D Imagine that you fought for the Romans in the battle shown in the picture. Describe the fight as if you were writing a diary or a letter the next day. These are some Roman men's names you could use: Marcus, Lucius, Gaius, Julius.

2 Hadrian's Wall

The signal beacons have been lit on Hadrian's Wall to warn that there is going to be an attack. Three Roman cavalrymen have news of the enemy and the guards in the milecastle are hurrying to their posts. Other soldiers are turning away some people who wish to go north into Caledonia (Scotland). A signal tower in the distance has lit its beacon and reinforcements are arriving along the road to the south of the wall.

The Emperor Hadrian ordered the wall to be built in the year AD 122 to be a boundary to the north of the Roman lands in Britain. Ever since then the Caledonians have attacked it now and again. The wall was seventy-two miles long and was built right across the north of Britain from Carlisle in the west to Wallsend on the River Tyne in the east. There were forts all along the wall and milecastles, like the one in the picture, every mile between the forts. Between the milecastles were signal turrets. You can still walk along parts of the wall today and see the remains of the forts, milecastles and turrets.

Things to do

A Write the heading **Hadrian's Wall** in your book and copy out this paragraph filling in the missing words.
The Emperor _____ gave orders for the wall to be built. It was started in the year AD _____. When it was finished it was _____ miles long and stretched from _____ in the west to _____ in the east. It was built as a _____ to mark the northern frontier of Roman Britain. The people who lived to the north of the wall were called _____

and they often attacked it. To defend the wall there were _____, and between these were _____, which were built every mile. There were also signal _____, which were used to give warning of attacks.

B Answer the following questions by looking at the picture.
1 Each milecastle could hold up to fifty or sixty men. How many soldiers can you see at this milecastle?
2 What has been made in front of the wall to slow up an enemy attack?
3 How can you tell that people travelled a lot across the frontier?
4 How could a warning of a night attack be passed along the wall?
5 Many Roman soldiers did not like serving on the wall. Can you think of any reasons for this?

C Draw a picture of the Caledonians attacking the wall. They would try to break down the door of a milecastle and climb over the wall. They would be dressed rather like the men of Boudicca's army.

D Imagine that you are a soldier on duty on the wall in the middle of winter. Write a letter home to your family (which could be in a warm country like Italy or Spain) complaining about your life on the wall.

8

3 A Roman Villa

When the Romans ruled Britain most people lived in the towns. Two Roman towns were Chester and York and there were many others. The food for the people in the towns came from farms in the countryside. The villa was like today's farmhouse. It was the centre of a farming estate. Many Romans lived in these villas, although the farmwork was done by Britons.

Some villas were very big and grand, while others were quite small and simple. It depended upon how rich the owner was. The picture shows a small villa, although the Roman owner is having an extension built. The villa has brick walls and a tile roof. The framework is made of wood. At the back of the villa is a bath-house and the whole building has a fence round it.

One of the new rooms will have central heating. You can see the piles of bricks on which the floor will rest. Next to it is the furnace room where a fire will be lit. The hot air from this will pass under the floor and heat the room. This sort of central heating system was called a hypocaust.

Things to do

A Write the heading **A Roman Villa** in your book. Copy out this paragraph and fill in the missing words.
A villa was like a modern _____. It was the centre of a farming _____. They supplied the Roman towns such as _____ and _____ with _____. Some of the rooms were heated by a _____, which was a sort of central heating. Some villas had a _____ because the Romans liked to keep themselves clean. The roofs were made of _____ and the framework was often made of _____. The work on the farm was done by _____.

B Answer the following questions by looking at the picture.
1 What sort of food do you think the Romans in this villa ate?
2 Why is there a fence round the villa?
3 How many ground floor rooms will the new extension have?
4 The man in the middle of the extension is making a mosaic floor? What is a mosaic?
5 What is the farmworker in the field in the distance doing? Can you see in the picture where he lives?

C Once you have found out what a mosaic is you could make one yourself. Try using small squares of coloured sticky paper to make a picture.

D Imagine that you are the owner of the villa in the picture. Your servant is serving you and your guests with a drink in the courtyard. Describe the villa to them and tell them about the new building work that is going on.

4 Saint Augustine

All his life King Ethelbert of Kent has believed in the old Saxon gods. Some of these gods were Woden (the chief god), Tiw (the god of war) and Thunor (the god of the air and thunder). Now he is listening to a strange man who has come to England to tell the Saxons about Christianity. Ethelbert's wife is Queen Bertha. She is already a Christian, but the king still does not trust the man in the long black robe. He will only listen to him outdoors where he thinks the man will not be able to use any magic on him.

The man's name is Augustine. He has been sent from Rome by Pope Gregory. His job is to make the Saxons give up their old gods and become Christians. He and a few other monks have only been in England for a short time. The year is AD 597. By the end of the year the King and many of his people will become Christians. After he died, Augustine was made a saint.

Things to do

A Write the heading **Saint Augustine** in your book. Copy out this paragraph and fill in the missing words.
In the year AD _____ Pope _____ sent a monk called Augustine to England. His job was to try and convert the English to _____. King _____ of Kent already had a Christian wife. Her name was _____. The King met _____ outdoors. He let him and the other _____ preach to his people. Soon many of the Saxons became Christians. They gave up believing in their old gods such as _____ and _____. Augustine was made a _____ after he died.

B Answer the following questions by looking at the picture.
1 How can you tell that Queen Bertha was a Christian?
2 Do the Saxons look as though they trust Augustine or not? Think of some reasons for your answer.
3 The Saxons did not have buttons or zips. How were their clothes fastened?
4 What might the king have used his large dog for, apart from guarding his house?
5 Augustine and the other monk both have tonsures. Use a dictionary to find out what a tonsure is.

C Saint Augustine was not the only person who tried to convert the people of the British Isles to Christianity. These are the names of some others. See if you can find out about them. Write a few lines about each of them:
Columba, Aidan, Patrick.

D King Ethelbert was not very happy about listening to Augustine at first! He was afraid that Augustine was a magician. Queen Bertha knew that her husband would not be harmed. Make up a conversation between them before their meeting with Augustine. Try to show how the Queen persuaded her husband that he had nothing to fear.

5 Vikings

A Viking longship is being loaded with supplies. Men are carrying sacks of food on board. Two others are bringing spears. Soon the longship will leave the village in the fiord and join other Viking ships. Together they will sail across the North Sea to attack the Saxons in England.

The leader of the Vikings is saying goodbye to his wife and son. Another man is telling him that the longship is almost ready to leave. It will be many weeks before they see their village again with its great longhouse and its carved runestone. Runes were stick-like letters and were thought to be magical.

The Vikings came from the countries we now call Norway, Denmark and Sweden. They were great sailors and soldiers. They sailed across the Atlantic Ocean and reached North America. Many came to live in England and became traders and farmers.

Things to do

A Write the heading **Vikings** in your book. Copy out this paragraph and fill in the missing words.

The Vikings came from Denmark, _____ and _____. They sailed across the _____ Sea to attack England. Some reached North _____ by sailing across the _____ Ocean. Their boats were called _____. The Vikings were very good _____ and they were fierce fighters. Their homes were in narrow bays called _____. They used magic letters called _____. They carved these on _____ and wood.

B Answer these questions by looking at the picture.
1 What is the boy giving to his father?
2 Name two ways in which the longship could be made to move.
3 Which three types of weapons can you see?
4 What do you think the carving on the prow (front) of the longship is?
5 Where are the Vikings' shields kept on the longship?

C Draw a picture of a Viking attack. Show them jumping from their longships onto the beach. Make sure that you make them look fierce with their helmets, shields and weapons.

D Copy or trace a map of Europe in your book. Mark on it the countries the Vikings came from and the places where they went. These are some of them:

England, Scotland, Ireland, France, Russia, Iceland, the Orkney and Shetland Islands.

Try to find out some other places they sailed to.

14

6 Alfred the Great

It is four years since King Alfred and his Saxon army defeated the Danish Vikings at the Battle of Edington. That was in the year AD 878. Now another Danish army is on the way. Alfred is going round his kingdom to make sure that his people are ready when the attack comes. His army is ready and so is his fleet of longships. Many towns have walls and deep ditches built round them to keep attackers out. These fortified towns are called burghs.

Alfred set up schools to teach people to read and write. He made new laws and had them written down for people to see. In the picture Alfred and some of his men are visiting a monastery where the monks are copying out Alfred's laws. Printing had not been invented and so all books had to be written by hand.

When the Danes did attack, Alfred defeated them again. He died in the year AD 899. He is the only English king to be called 'the Great'.

Things to do

A Write the heading **Alfred the Great** in your book. Copy out this paragraph and fill in the missing words.

King Alfred the _____ defeated the Vikings at the Battle of _____ in the year AD _____. To protect England from another attack he built fortified towns called _____ and built a fleet of _____. Alfred made new _____ and had them written for all to see. He set up _____ where the monks taught people to _____ and _____. They copied books out by hand because _____ had not yet been invented.

B Answer these questions by looking at the picture.
1 What is Alfred wearing to show that he is the king?
2 What is the object on top of the writing desk?
3 What are the monks using to write with?
4 How did the penknife get its name?
5 What are the soldiers wearing to protect their bodies?

C Before Alfred defeated the Danes in AD 878 he had to hide from them for a time. He hid near a place called Athelney in Somerset. There is a story told about him and some cakes while he was there. Try to find out what this story was and tell it in your own words.

D Alfred and the Danes divided England between them. The Danes lived in the eastern part of the country. It was called the Danelaw. Many towns in this part of England were started by the Danes. Some of their names end with the letters -by or -thorpe. Using an atlas, make a list of towns in eastern England ending in this way.

7 The Battle of Hastings

King Harold of England and what is left of his Saxon army stand behind a wall of shields on top of Senlac Hill near Hastings. It is late in the afternoon of 14th October 1066, and the battle has been going on all day long.

Harold chose to fight on foot and let Duke William of Normandy and his army charge up the hill on their horses to attack him. Now the Norman knights are charging again for the last time, for in this charge King Harold and his men will be killed. The shield wall of Harold's housecarls (bodyguard) will be broken and a Norman sword will cut down the last Saxon king of England.

The Battle of Hastings put an end to the quarrel between Harold and William about who was to be the ruler of England. William marched on from Hastings to London, where he was crowned King of England on Christmas Day, 1066, in Westminster Abbey.

Things to do

A   Write the heading **The Battle of Hastings** in your book and copy out this paragraph filling in the missing words.
In the year _____, Duke William of _____ invaded England. His soldiers fought a battle on _____ Hill near Hastings against King _____ of England. The English king and his _____, or bodyguard, were all killed in the fight. He was the last _____ king to rule this country. William then went to _____ where he was crowned king in _____ Abbey on _____ Day.

B   Answer these questions by looking at the picture.
1   What weapons do Harold's men have?
2   How many Saxons have been wounded by arrows?
3   How are the Normans using their lances?
4   How are the heavy shields held in place?
5   What do you think the picture is on Harold's standard (flag)?

C   Draw a picture of a soldier of this time. Label these things in your picture:
   Two-handed axe, kite-shaped shield, hauberk (coat of chain mail), helmet with nasal (to protect the face).

D   The story of the quarrel between Harold and William and the Battle of Hastings is shown on the Bayeux Tapestry, which was sewn very soon after 1066. It is a sort of cloth strip-cartoon. Find a book with pictures of the tapestry in and use it to help you make up your own strip cartoon of the events of 1066.

8 A Medieval Village

The people who live in this small medieval village are harvesting. They are cutting the corn and ploughing the land. The land is divided into strips and each man farms his own strips. The fields are big and open. There are no hedges like today. When the corn has been made ready it will be taken to the miller. He is standing by the windmill on top of the hill. There it will be ground to make flour.

The lord of the manor lives in the manor house by the river. He owns all the land in the village. The people in the village do his work for him. In return he lets them use his land to grow their own food. They also have to give one tenth (a tithe) of all they grow to the church. This food is kept in the tithe barn by the church.

In the Middle Ages most people in England lived in villages and worked on the land. There were no factories and very few large towns and cities.

Things to do

A Write the heading **A Medieval Village** in your book. Copy out this paragraph and fill in the missing words.
In the _____ Ages most people lived in _____ and worked on the _____. The land was owned by the _____ of the manor. The fields were open and did not have _____ round them. They were divided into _____. The corn was ground into _____ in a _____. The people gave some of their crops to the church. This was known as a _____. This food was kept in a _____ _____.

B Answer these questions by looking at the picture.
1 How many different kinds of animals can you see in the village?
2 The top part of the windmill can be turned round. Why?
3 The lord of the manor is shown coming home. Where do you think he has been?
4 How were the stocks used to punish people?
5 If the village was attacked by soldiers or outlaws where could the people go to be safe? (There is more than one place.)

C Match these different things in the village to the numbers on the picture.
Church, Tithe barn, Stocks, Windmill, Manor House, Pound (where stray animals were kept), Plough, Bridge, Packhorses, Common land (where people could graze their animals).

D Draw a plan of a medieval village in your book. Label the different things in the village in your drawing. You could use the village in the picture for your plan.

9 Attacking a Castle

In the Middle Ages castles were built to keep enemies out. They had high, thick walls and often had a moat round the outside which might be filled with water. To capture a castle soldiers had to climb over the walls or break a hole in them. Sometimes they could not do this. Then they surrounded the castle and waited until the people inside ran out of food and had to give in. This was called a siege.

The soldiers in the picture are trying to get into the castle. They are trying to get over the walls by using scaling ladders and two big siege-towers. They are also trying to break down the walls. The machine in the front of the picture is called a mangonel. It throws large stones at the walls. At the right is another stone-throwing machine called a trebuchet. The soldiers are also using a battering-ram.

Things to do

A Write the heading **Attacking a Castle** in your book. Copy out this paragraph and fill in the missing words.
Castles had high _____ and often had a _____ filled with water to keep enemies out. Attackers tried to break down the walls. They used _____-rams and stone-throwing machines called _____ and _____. They also tried to climb over the walls by using _____ ladders and _____-towers. If this did not work they would wait until the people inside the _____ ran out of food. This was called a _____.

B Answer these questions by looking at the picture.
1 Why are some soldiers standing behind wooden boards?
2 How are the people inside the castle trying to stop the attackers from getting in?
3 What are the attackers using to fire arrows at the castle?
4 The siege-towers are covered in wet cowhides. What did this stop the soldiers in the castle from doing to them? (A clue is that the siege-towers were made out of wood.)
5 What have the attackers done to get across the moat?

C Copy or trace a map of Britain into your book. Mark on it these places where there are famous castles:
Dover, Warwick, Conway, Stirling, Kenilworth, Harlech, Caernarvon.

D Imagine that you are a soldier in a castle under attack. Describe how the attackers try to break in and how you try to keep them out.

10 A Medieval Tournament

A young squire hands his master his helmet. Another squire holds his lance. In a few minutes the knight will be taking part in a joust. Like the other two knights in the picture he will charge down the field and try to knock another man off his horse. This was called jousting.

This was a favourite sport of soldiers in the Middle Ages. It meant that they could keep in training for battles when there was no war. These meetings where jousting and other sports took place were called tournaments. The one in the picture is taking place in the grounds of a castle. It is being watched by people who are sitting in a special stand.

At the left of the picture another knight and a lady are standing by a quintain. Knights could charge at this with their lances and try to hit the shield. When they did this the top of the quintain swung round and the weight on the other end hit them if they were not careful.

Also in the picture are the tents where the knights got changed and ready for the tournament.

Things to do

A Write the heading **A Medieval Tournament** in your book. Copy out this paragraph and fill in the missing words.
Knights practised fighting at contests called _____.
Each knight had a _____ who helped him to get ready. When two knights charged at each other holding a _____ this was known as _____. The idea was to knock the other knight off his _____. Each knight carried a _____ to protect himself and wore a _____ on his head. People sat in a _____ to watch the contest. Sometimes knights charged at a _____. This was a post with a shield at one side and a _____ at the other side.

B Answer these questions by looking at the picture.
1 Why do the knights have pictures on their shields?
2 The man in the centre of the picture is taking part in another sport. What is it?
3 Name the weapons the squire at the left of the picture is cleaning.
4 How are the horses kept apart during the jousting?
5 How can the knight see and breathe when he has his helmet on?

C Draw a picture of a knight jousting. Make up your own picture for his shield and a pattern for his tunic. You can colour the covering for his horse the same way.

D Imagine that television had been invented in the Middle Ages. Pretend that you are a sports commentator and describe a jousting contest like they do today for football and cricket matches.

11 A Medieval Pilgrimage

The picture shows a group of people on their way to visit a holy shrine. They are pilgrims and the journey they are making is called a pilgrimage. A shrine was a place where holy objects like the bones of a saint were kept. People in the Middle Ages travelled to these places to pray. Some went to give thanks for something good that had happened to them, or to pray for good luck, or to be cured of an illness. One of the most famous shrines was at Canterbury Cathedral where Saint Thomas à Becket had been killed.

A man called Geoffrey Chaucer, who lived from 1340 to 1400, wrote about a group of pilgrims on their way to Canterbury. They all told stories to pass the time on their journey. Chaucer's book is called *The Canterbury Tales*.

A monk rides at the head of the pilgrims in the picture and behind him are a knight and a nun. The knight wears a sword and a small shield called a buckler. Next come two merchants who are busy talking. They have not noticed the man on foot at the right of the picture, but the two walkers and the priest and the squire at the back of the group have. The man is a leper and those who have seen him are scared of him.

Things to do

A Write the heading **A Medieval Pilgrimage** in your books and copy out this paragraph filling in the missing words. In the _____ Ages many people went on journeys called _____. They went to pray at holy places or _____. Some prayed to be _____ of an illness while others prayed for good _____. A famous holy place was at _____ Cathedral where Thomas à _____ had been killed. Geoffrey _____ wrote a book about a pilgrimage. It was called The _____. He died in the year _____.

B Answer these questions by looking at the picture.
1 Why do you think pilgrims travelled in groups rather than on their own? Their weapons will give you a clue.
2 What disease does the leper have? Why is he ringing a bell?
3 What do you think the peasant at the left of the picture is praying in front of?
4 The countryside today does not look much like that in the picture. What is missing in the picture that you see growing in the countryside today?
5 The pilgrims stayed at inns each night and did not camp out in the open. How can you tell this from the picture?

C Copy or trace a map of England into your book. Using an atlas, mark on the map the following places which had churches or cathedrals where people went on pilgrimages.
Canterbury (Kent), Westminster (London), Durham (Northumberside), Bury St Edmunds (Suffolk), St Albans (Hertfordshire).

D You might like to make up a story about a modern group of people on a pilgrimage just like Geoffrey Chaucer did in the fourteenth century. Decide what sort of people are in your group and make up a short story for each of them to tell as they travel along.

12 Joan of Arc

English soldiers armed with halberds keep a French crowd back. Behind them another soldier chains a young French girl to a wooden stake, round which is piled firewood. Her name is Joan of Arc and she is just nineteen years old. Soon the people of Rouen will see her burned to death. She has asked for a cross and an English soldier has made one from two sticks and is holding it up for her to see. The date is 29th May 1431.

The English had been fighting the French ever since 1337 when King Edward III of England said that he should be king of France as well. The English won many battles until Joan of Arc led the French army. Then the French began to win.

Joan came from the small village of Domrémy and she said that she had heard angels telling her that she must lead the French against the English. She had dressed in men's clothes and had lived like a soldier. She was captured in 1430 and was handed over to the English. They said that she was a witch and put her on trial. After her death the French kept on fighting and defeated the English. This long war was known as The Hundred Years' War.

Things to do

A Write the heading **Joan of Arc** in your book. Copy out this paragraph and fill in the missing words.
Joan of Arc was born in the village of _____ in the country of _____. The _____ Years' War was being fought in France at that time. Joan said that _____ told her to fight the English. With her in charge the French began to win. She was _____ in 1430. The English said that she was a _____ and put her on _____. She was burnt at the stake in the town of _____ in the year _____. Later, the French _____ the English.

B Answer these questions by looking at the picture.
1 Why are the English soldiers keeping the crowds back?
2 What is being used to tie Joan to the stake, and why?
3 What has the red cross on the soldiers' tunics got to do with England?
4 How many men will set light to the firewood?
5 Why has the fire been built well away from the buildings?

C Find out more about the story of Joan of Arc. Copy or trace a map of France and mark on it the following places:
Domrémy, Orleans, Rheims, Compiègne, Rouen.
Write a few lines about how each of these places played a part in the story of Joan.

D Imagine that you were in the market place at Rouen when Joan was burned at the stake. Describe what you saw and how you felt about it. This will depend on whether you are English or French.

13 Printing

William Caxton stands at the right of the picture. He is reading one of the new books his shop has just made. The book is special. It is one of the first books to be printed in England. The year is 1476 and Caxton has just opened his printing shop in London. The Chinese invented printing, but the first man to use it in Europe was John Gutenberg of Germany. He printed his first book about twenty-five years before Caxton opened his shop in London.

The man in the centre of the picture is checking the first copy of a printed page for any mistakes. Behind him another man holds the lever of the printing press, while a third man waits to put ink on the type (the letters which will print the page). In the background is a man called a compositor. It is his job to take the letters out of the case in front of him to make up the words to be printed. He puts them all together to make each page.

Before this time all books had to be written by hand. This meant that there were not many books and it took a very long time for copies to be made. Printing changed all that. Books could be printed faster than being written. This made them cost less and it was easier to print lots of copies. Because there were more books, more people learned to read. News spread more quickly and ideas could reach more people.

Things to do

A   Write the heading **Printing** in your book. Copy out this paragraph and fill in the missing words.
William _____ brought printing to England in the year _____. He opened a shop in _____. The _____ had invented printing and the first man to use it in Europe was John _____ of _____. Before this time all books had to be written by _____. This took a long _____ and made books expensive and rare. Printing changed all that. Because of printing more people learned to _____ and _____ spread more quickly.

B   Answer these questions by looking at the picture.
1   How is the printing press raised and lowered?
2   Why is it important to check the first page to be printed?
3   What is the man using to put ink on the type?
4   What are the printers wearing to protect their clothes?
5   How can you tell that some printing mistakes have been made in the shop that day?

C   Try printing your own initials by using a potato. Cut the potato in half and carve the letters on the cut sides. Remember to carve the letters *backwards*. Paint the flat parts of the cut sides and press them down on a clean piece of paper.

D   Besides books and newspapers, printing is used in many ways today. We could not do without it. Make a list of some of the things on which you can see printing. Look around your school and your home.

14 The Battle of Bosworth

William Brandon, who carries the red dragon flag of Henry Tudor, is one second away from death. In a moment he will be killed by the lance of King Richard III, who is riding the white horse. Richard has charged with his knights down Ambion Hill near the town of Market Bosworth in Leicestershire. He is trying to reach Henry Tudor at the right of the picture, who has drawn his sword to protect himself.

In the background the footsoldiers and archers of the two armies are fighting, but they will not decide who wins the battle. On top of Ambion Hill, at the left of the picture, are more of King Richard's army. They are led by the Duke of Northumberland, but they will not join in the fight. Henry Tudor is trying to reach some more soldiers, who are led by Sir William Stanley. Stanley is supposed to fight for Richard, but in a short while he will change sides and join Henry.

Richard was killed in this battle, which took place on 22nd August 1485. Henry Tudor became King Henry VII of England after the battle and he ruled for twenty-four years. It took him many years to make England peaceful but when he died his son, Henry VIII, became king without any trouble or fighting.

Things to do

A Write the heading **The Battle of Bosworth** in your books. Copy out this paragraph and fill in the missing words.

The Battle of _____ was fought in the year _____. It was fought on _____ Hill in the county of _____. King Richard III was killed and Henry _____ became king of England. Two of the men who should have fought for Richard were the Duke of _____ and Sir William _____, but they betrayed him. Henry VII ruled for _____ years and died in the year _____. His son became King _____ VIII.

B Answer the following questions by looking at the picture.
1 Name the different types of weapons being used in the battle.
2 What is Richard wearing to show that he is the king?
3 What are the ways Richard could tell which man in armour was Henry Tudor? (William Brandon holds one clue.)
4 Which parts of the horses are protected by armour?
5 Look closely at the men's armour. Which parts of the body are the least protected?

C Draw the White Boar standard of King Richard with its red and blue background, and the Red Dragon standard of Henry Tudor with its green and white background. Both standards have the red cross of St George and England.

D Imagine that there were newspapers in 1485. Make up a front-page story for the day after the battle. Invent a headline and write a short account of the fighting. You could draw a picture in black and white to make it look like a photograph.

Places to Visit

Roman Britain

There is nothing to see of Boudicca's last fight at Mancetter but the *Lunt Roman Fort* at *Baginton* near Coventry was built at the time of the revolt. The Fort has been partly reconstructed and there is a small museum there. *Chedworth Villa* (off the A429 north of Cirencester) is worth a visit, as is the site at *Fishbourne* near Chichester. This has wonderful mosaics but was a palace rather than a villa. *Hadrian's Wall* was built right across the country, but the best place to see it now is at *Housesteads Fort* (off the A69 east of Hexham).

Saxon England

There are not very many Saxon buildings left to see because so many of them were made of wood and this has rotted away. The church at *Greenstead* in Essex is still largely Saxon and the stone Church of St Laurence at *Bradford-on-Avon* in Wiltshire was built in Saxon times. At *Coppergate* in *York* the remains of a Viking settlement have been excavated and many of the finds can be seen in the *County Museum* in *York*.

Medieval England

There is an 11th century ruined abbey at *Battle*, north of Hastings, on the site of the battle of 1066. A medieval open-field system can still be seen at *Laxton* (near the junction of the A1 and A6075 in Nottinghamshire). There are castles all over Britain but *Warwick Castle* is not ruined and has a good collection of armour. The best collections of armour and weapons can be seen in the *Tower of London* and the *Wallace Collection* at Manchester Square in London.

The site of the Battle of Bosworth of 1485 is open to the public. The Battlefield Centre near *Market Bosworth* in Leicestershire has a small museum and film theatre. Visitors can walk round the battlefield on a special trail.

These are just a few suggestions of places to visit connected with the subjects in this book. If you want to find out more you should visit your nearest museum to have a look at their collections of objects. Your local library will also be able to help you to find out more information.